Call Me Vicky

by Nicola & Stacey Bland

Published by Playdead Press 2019

© Nicola Bland and Stacey Bland 2019

Nicola Bland and Stacey Bland have asserted their rights under the Copyright, Design and Patents Act, 1988, to be identified as the authors of this work.

A CIP catalogue record for this book is available from the British Library.

ISBN 978-1-910067-74-1

Caution

All rights whatsoever in this play are strictly reserved and application for performance should be sought through the author before rehearsals begin. No performance may be given unless a license has been obtained.

This book is sold subject to the condition that it shall not by way of trade or otherwise, be lent, resold, hired out, or otherwise circulated without the publisher's prior consent in any form of binding or cover other than that in which it is published and without a similar condition including this condition being imposed on the subsequent purchaser.

Playdead Press
www.playdeadpress.com

Call Me Vicky

By Nicola and Stacey Bland

Call Me Vicky was performed at the Pleasance Theatre, Islington from 19th February to 9th March 2019 with the following team:

Cast List: (*In order of Appearance*)

Sylvie	**Wendi Peters**
Debbie	**Nicola Bland**
Vicky	**Matt Greenwood**
Fat Pearl	**Ben Welch**
Gabby	**Stacey Victoria Bland**
Sid	**Adam Young**

Creatives:

Writers	**Nicola Bland and Stacey Bland**
Director & Dramaturg	**Victoria Gimby**
Lighting Designer	**Holly Ellis**
Sound Designer	**Jac Cooper**
Set & Costume Designer	**Martha Hegarty**
Company Stage Manager	**Karan Sidhu**
Producer	**Post-It Productions**
Consulting Producer	**Marcus Ellard**
Additional Casting	**Pearson Casting**
PR	**Chloe Nelkin Consultancy**
Assistant Director	**Jordan Carter**
Set & Costume Assistant	**Kerri Woods**

CAST

Wendi Peters | Sylvie (*She / Her*)

Wendi is best known for her role as Cilla Battersby Brown in Coronation Street – a role that she played for over four years, and returned to for a stint in 2014 after seven years away. Her portrayal of this much loved character has led to appearances on many television programmes including *Celebrity Sewing Bee for Children in Need, Pointless Celebrities, Keep it in the Family, Celebrity Mastermind, Adrenaline Junkie with Jack Osbourne, The F Word with Gordon Ramsay* and *Celebrity Masterchef*, in which she reached the finals. Wendi plays the recurring character Cook Jenkins in *Hetty Feather* (BBC).

Other TV includes: *Hacker Time, Sadie J; Out of the Blue* and *Cardiac Arrest* (BBC); *Crime Stories, Bad Girls* (ITV).

Film includes: *Gyppo*; Cilla in *Coronation St - Out of Africa* and Emily in *In Love and War*.

Theatre includes: Most recently Wendi could be seen in the *Salad Days, Quartet, Wonderland* and *Oh What a Lovely War* (National Tours); *Hatched 'n' Dispatched* (Park Theatre); her one-woman show *Let Me Sing And I'm Happy* (St James Theatre); Melissa Frake in *State Fair* for London Musical Theatre Orchestra (Cadogan Hall, London); *Frank and Friends – A Concert with Frank Wildhorn* (Palace Theatre, Manchester); *Rutherford & Sons* (National Tour); Kath Casey in *Our House 10th Anniversary Concert* directed by Matthew Warchus (Savoy, London); *The Mystery of Edwin Drood* (Arts Theatre, West End); *April in Paris* directed by John Godber (Hull Truck, National Tour); *The Game* for Northern Broadsides directed by Barrie Rutter (National Tour); *Grumpy Old Women Live 2 – Chin up Britain* (National Tour & Novello Theatre, West End); *Vagina Monologues* (National Tour); *Mrs Whippy* – one woman play written by Cecelia

Ahern (Dublin & National Tour, Ireland); *Vagina Monologues* (Tivoli Theatre, Dublin); *Snow White* (Orchard Theatre, Dartford); *Children Will Listen – celebrating Stephen Sondheim's 75th Birthday* (Theatre Royal, Drury Lane); *Follies in Concert* (London Palladium); *Me and My Girl*; *Murder on the Nile*; *Cinderella*; *Noises Off*; *Bedroom Farce* (Palace Theatre, Westcliff); *Teechers* (Hull Truck National Tour); *Scarlet Pimpernel*; *Into The Woods* (Wolsey Theatre, Ipswich); *A Slice of Saturday Night* (Playhouse, Derby); *Grease* (Olympia Theatre, Dublin); *Sugar*; *Gypsy* (West Yorkshire Playhouse, Leeds); *Guys and Dolls*, *Hello Dolly* (National Tours).

Radio include: *BBC Radio 2's Friday Night is Music Night* (guest soloist).

Wendi loves cooking and baking and has started a blog diary, recording her recipes and kitchen exploits; *www.wendipeterspuddingqueen.blogspot.com*.

For more information, please visit www.intertalentgroup.com

Nicola Bland | Debbie (*She / Her*)

Nicola began professionally acting from a young age with her first lead role in the film *Yellow* starring alongside Ray Winstone, shortly followed by Eponine in *Les Miserables* at The Palace Theatre. Since leaving E15 Acting School, Nicola went straight into *Tits/Teeth* at the Soho Theatre and has since been working on various projects.

Theatre includes: *Tales of Aviation Heroes* (Soho Theatre); *I Vow to Thee My Country* (Roundhouse Theatre); *Reserves* (Criterion Theatre); *Monsters* (Barbican Cockpit); *Concrete Fairground* (Royal Court Theatre) and most recently *Fight Club* which transferred to Hong Kong after a sell-out run in London.

TV and Film includes: *Pickles, The Bill* (ITV); *Casualty, Messiah* (BBC).

Nicola is excited to be playing the role of Debbie and watching her play come to life.

Matt Greenwood | Vicky (*He / Him / His*)

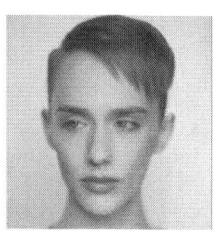

Matt has trained at the following institutions from the age of 6 years old up until the present, and still has regular coaching from acting and dialect coach Mark Hudson: Manchester School of Acting, National Youth Theatre, The Manchester College – Shena Simon Campus, Carol Godby Theatre Workshop, and the Helen O'Grady Children's Drama Academy.

TV includes: *Giri / Haji* (BBC / Netflix); *The A Word* (BBC / SundanceTV); *Casualty & Waterloo Road* (BBC).

Film includes: *Bohemian Rhapsody* (20th Century Fox).

Theatre includes: *Voya & Goliath, A Midsummer Night's Dream* (National Youth Theatre); *Hand To God* (Royal Northern College of Music); *Jerusalem, Actor* by Steven Berkoff, *Posh* (Waterside Theatre); *Success, The Caucasian Chalk Circle, Port* (Sackville Theatre); *Care* (Carol Godby Theatre), *Romeo and Juliet* (Library Theatre Manchester), *Du Temps En Temps, Tell* (The Met Theatre).

Workshops include: *Timeless / Twelfth Night* with Rikki Beadle-Blair (National Youth Theatre).

Ben Welch | Fat Pearl (*He /Him / His*)

Ben Welch trained at the BAFTA award winning Television Workshop in Nottingham.

Theatre credits include: *Mythic* (Charing Cross Theatre); *Jack Rooke's Happy Hour* (Soho Theatre); *The Leftovers*

(Curve Theatre / Sheep Soup Productions); *Big Sister Little Brother* (The Spark Arts), *Mrs Green* (Nottingham Playhouse / Edinburgh Fringe); *The Invention Of Acting*, *A Handbag Darkly* (Edinburgh Fringe).

TV and Film includes: *Project X* (Hatrick Productions); *Gangsta Wraps* (Dealmaker); *Commando* (Sheep Soup Productions).

He is a founding member of the theatre company Sheep Soup Productions.

Stacey Victoria Bland | Gabby (*She / Her*)

Training: London School of Musical Theatre, National Youth Theatre.

Theatre includes: *Call Me Vicky* (Theatre Royal Stratford East); *Don't Dress For Dinner* (UK Tour); *Aladdin* (Polka-Dot Pantomimes); *The Day of the Funfair* (Redbridge Drama Centre); *Santa's New Sleigh* (UK Tour, Arts Theatre London); *Cinderella* (Lichfield Garrick); *Home Theatre* (Theatre Royal Stratford East); *Finian's Rainbow* (Union Theatre); *Hey Mr Producer* (Lyceum); *Oliver* (Palladium); *GamePlan* (Hen and Chickens); *Between Ten and Six* (Brighton Fringe); *Little Red Riding Hood* (Theatre Royal Stratford East); *Into The Woods* (Bridewell Theatre); *Falariki: The Greek Tragedy* (Lyric Hammersmith); *Tales of Aviation Heroes* (Soho Theatre); *Yeoman of the Guard* (Tower of London Festival); *God Save the Teen* (Trafalgar Square); *Blade Runner* (Secret Cinema, Canary Wharf) and *Bugsy Malone* (Secret Cinema, The Troxy).

TV and Film includes: Stacey has been in ad campaigns for *Now TV: The Walking Dead; Green Flag; Wotsits; Nokia; ASDA* and *Kellogs*. Female lead in short film *Best Bud* (Sanbon Films); *'Coulda Shoulda Woulda'* (London Dreams Motion Pictures); *Downsizing* (Mad Ninja Films) and most recently Juliet in the pilot for *Mind Makeover Challenge*. She was a regular dancer on *The Justin Lee Collins Show* (ITV2) as well as dancing for *Sky Sports*, *The Katy Brand Show* (ITV2) and One Direction for *X Factor* (ITV).

Stacey cannot wait to share *Call Me Vicky* with you all and thanks her Sister and Co-Writer Nicola, without whom none of this would be possible.

Adam Young | Sid (*He* / *Him* / *His*)

Adam is a member of The National Youth Theatre and graduated from Mountview Academy of Theatre Arts in 2017. In his final year he was chosen to represent the school as part of The Sam Wanamaker Festival. Later he reprised his role of Face in *The Alchemist*, at the Shakespeare Festival – The Globe Theatre, Neuss.

This autumn he made his screen debut at the Edinburgh International Film Festival in the new British film *Two for Joy*, starring alongside Billie Piper, Samantha Morton and Daniel Mays. He is soon to appear in the new comedy Netflix series *Sex Education*.

Other credits include: *Henry V* (The Petersfield Shakespeare Festival); *DMC* (N16 Theatre); *Nu Media* (Television Pilot).

CREATIVE

Victoria Gimby | Director & Dramaturg
(*She / Her*)

Victoria works as a director, writer and dramaturg having trained at both Mountview Academy of Theatre Arts (BA) and RADA / Birkbeck University (MA Text and Performance).

As Associate Director: *Rock of Ages* (UK Tour, Nick Winston); *Myth: The Rise and Fall of Orpheus* (The Other Palace Theatre, Arlene Phillips); and *27 The Musical* (Cockpit Theatre).

As Assistant Director: *Zanna Don't!* (Entourage Prod, The Landor); *The Mikado* (Entourage Prod, The RISE Leicester Square).

As Director: *News Revue* (The Canal Cafe Theatre); *The Ballad of Paragon Station* (International Tour incl Gilded Balloon, Hull Truck Theatre, Lyttelton Arts Festival New Zealand); *Jam Jars* (The Actors Centre); *Luck of the Draw* (Charterhouse Prod, RADA Festival 2016); Variety Shows for Hapag Lloyd Cruises; *UKIP! The Musical* (Movement Director, winner of THE STAGE award for Ensemble Excellence, Waterloo East, Ed Festival).

As a Playwright: *Zelda* (Musical Workshop, The Other Palace); *Rosa* (Musical Workshop); *By Virtue Fall* (Winner of LOST Theatre One Act Festival – The LOST Theatre/The Space Theatre); *Pieces of Eight* (RADA Festival/Stanley Halls Invention Festival); *Forget me not* (The Vaults, Waterloo), *A Little bit of Dickens* (Hertford Theatre/Jamie Oliver's Feastival/Edinburgh Fringe); *A Little Bit of Rodgers and Hammerstein* (Hertford Theatre), *Alba Ur* (RADA).

As Dramaturg: *Myth: The Rise and Fall of Orpheus* (The Other Palace, Arlene Phillips), *Jam Jars* (The Actors Centre), *A Midsummer Night's Dream* (St Leonards-on-Sea Festival),

Butter (Winner of Outstanding New Work Award at The Vaults, Waterloo),

Victoria has worked as a reader for various theatres including The National Theatre and the Finborough and freelances as a tutor at SLP, RADA and Urdang. She was recently shortlisted for the Northern Writers' Awards 2018.

Martha Hegarty | Set & Costume Designer (She / Her)

Since graduating with an MA in Art History, Theory & Criticism, Martha has worked in various creative fields in Ireland and Vietnam. As well as set and costume design, she is involved in art writing, art education, illustration and painting. She is currently based in London as a graphic designer.

Holly Ellis | Lighting Designer (She / Her)

Holly trained at LAMDA. She has worked on *LadyBones, Nikoloas the Wonderkid, Thomas* (Vaults Festival 2019); *Anomaly* (Old Red Lion); *Jeannie* (Finborough); Borderline (Lion and Unicorn), *Sexy Laundry* (Tabard Theatre); *Schrodinger's Dog* (White Bear Theatre); *That Girl* (Old Red Lion); *Vanishing Man* and *Extinction Event* (High Tide & Pleasance Edinburgh 2018); *Sparks* (As Associate LD, High Tide & Pleasance Edinburgh 2018); *Conquest* (Bunker Theatre); *War Plays* (Tristan Bates Theatre); *Cream Tea and Incest* (Hope Theatre); *Much Ado About Nothing, Twelfth Night, Comedy of Errors* (Karamel Club, Mountview). Please see her website at www.hollyellislighting.com.

Jac Cooper | Sound Designer (He / Him / His)

Since graduating from the Bristol Old Vic Theatre School in 2016, Jac has worked as a Sound Designer and Composer in London, Edinburgh, Amsterdam and Dublin. Notable work includes *Caterpillar* (Theatre 503, Stephen Joseph Theatre), *Locked Up* (Tristan Bates Theatre), *True Cuts* (Bush Theatre Studio, Imperial College Festival, Amsterdam Medical

Conference), *Nest* (The Vaults), *All That We Found Here* (New Theatre Dublin), and *Snapshot* (Hope Theatre Islington).

Karan Sidhu – Company Stage Manager (He / Him / His)

Karan trained in Production Stage Management at the Royal Central School of Speech and Drama, University of London.

Theatre credits include working for English National Opera, Royal National Theatre, Punchdrunk Theatre Company, MJE Productions, PolkaDot Productions, Trinity London, Millennium Performing Arts, Garrick Theatre, Fortune Theatre, Queen's Theatre, Thameside Theatre, Embassy Theatre and Cochrane Theatre.

Television credits include working for Channel 4, ITV 2, Sky 1, Blast! Films, Mentorn Media, Studio Lambert, Betty and Buccaneer Media.

Marcus Ellard | Consulting Producer (He / Him / His)

Marcus has been working professionally since graduating as an actor from Drama Centre London in 2007.

He built up extensive experience in acting, directing and casting primarily at Theatre Royal Stratford East where he became an Associate Artist under then artistic director Kerry Michael. Whilst working as an associate artist at Theatre Royal Stratford East Marcus assisted with producing both new writing performances, musicals and readings.

In 2016 Marcus developed his experience and passion for the industry by becoming an agent and now works for InterTalent Rights Group.

Pearson Casting | Additional Casting

Headed up by husband and wife team, James and Rosie Pearson, are international freelance Casting Director based in Liverpool who work across all genres of entertainment. James and Rosie are both members of The Casting Directors Association.

Recent credits include –

Film & TV: Pearson Casting are currently working on: a new full-length feature, *Fetch* – Hurricane Films, Short Film, *Mummy's Boy* – Typecast Productions and Web Series, *Discretion* – DLW Productions. This year they assisted Jill Trevelick on a four part ITV drama, *Anne* (Children's Casting) as well as casting *Wormfood* – Ali Coulson / Sarah Higgins and *Power of Numbers* – Standard Chartered / Liverpool FC (Featuring Steven Gerrard).

Theatre: *Call Me Vicky* (Additional Casting) – The Pleasance Theatre, London; *Six The Musical* (Additional Casting) – The Arts Theatre, London; *Club Mex* – The Hope Mill Theatre, Manchester; *One Man's Story* – Liverpool Philharmonic Hall; *Bark* (Additional Casting) – C Venues, Edinburgh; *Myth: The Rise and Fall of Orpheus* – Directed by Arlene Phillips, The Other Palace, London; *Spellz* – UK Tour; *Aladdin Goes Pop* – UK Tour; *Cartoon Network Live* – South African, Indian & Middle Eastern Tour; *Beauty & The Beast* – The Black E, Liverpool; *Heaven On Earth* – UK Arena Tour, (starring Kerry Ellis); *Anything Goes* – (6 Offie Nominations) Upstairs At The Gatehouse, London; *Adam, Eve & Steve* – Kings Head, London & C Venues, Edinburgh; *The Return of Neverland* – UK Tour; *A Christmas Carol* starring Paul Nicholas – Winter Gardens; *Legally Blonde The Musical* – Aberystwyth Arts Centre.

Pearson Casting are also the UK Casting Directors for RWS Entertainment Group for Holland America Line, casting their principal production vocalists and dancers. They also look after Norwegian Cruise Line, Oceana Cruise Line and Regent Seven Sea, having cast *Rock of Ages*; *Legally Blonde*; *Shout! The Mod Musical*; *The Look of Love*; *Paradis*; *Burn The Floor*; *Wine Lovers The Musical*; and *Vegas The Show!* for Norwegian Creative Studios as well as being responsible for finding their UK based productions vocalists and dancers. Pearson Casting also work with Talent Artistic Group as their in-house casting team, looking after their casting for Haven Parks and TUI Sensatori Resorts Worldwide.

Director's Note

Call me Vicky is based on the true story of Vicky, a close family friend of sisters Stacey and Nicola Bland. The play has been in development long before I became attached and I was immediately impressed by how they had approached not only the subject matter, but writing about the life of a real person. As a writer of historical figures myself I have experienced the weight and responsibility that comes with telling someone else's story. I have discovered that, often, the closer you are to the person the story is about, the harder it can be to gain objectivity. In translating this story to the stage, Stacey and Nicola have taken great care in ensuring that the right people have been involved in the process by developing with audiences and actors from the transgender community and working with their families. Most importantly they have been given the full blessing from the woman herself, Vicky.

Stacey and Nicola are joining that growing band of 'herstory' writers; telling women's stories from history and giving a voice to those who, in the past, have been voiceless. This story is especially significant as this particular woman used to be a man.

Statistics in gender variance are notoriously poor because there is no way of monitoring it; many people live as transgender without registering as the legal process to change gender is complicated, medically intrusive and expensive. Even then, what it means to be transgender or to transition varies from person to person. Saying this (potentially due to increase in visibility of transgender people in the media and popular culture) these numbers have increased, yet in theatre, television and film transgender stories are still in short supply. This lack of representation has created a mystery surrounding the transgender community for those outside it and is something we were keen to address in our play.

Call Me Vicky is a play for the transgender community and for anyone battling with identity of any kind. We hope Vicky's story might shed some light on the judgement, discrimination and violence experienced daily by people who are brave enough to accept and live as who they really are, and that it will encourage other similar stories to find platforms.

When we meet Vicky in the play, she already knows and has accepted who she is and is saving for her first major operation. Although her internal battle with identity has been conquered to a degree, it is the external battles thrust upon her which make her question her place in the world. In a way, this play is a coming of age story for the world, and aims to spread a message of hope. Yes, we have come a long way since Vicky's journey through 1980's Soho, but we still have a very, very long way to go.

ADDITIONAL THANKS

Thanks to everyone who has helped from the conception to the realisation of this project; everyone who came to and performed in our fundraisers; Kitty Scott Claus, Ophelia Love, Crystal, Ruby Violet, Poppycock, Kate Playdon, Above the Arts Cabaret Club. Mysty Parks and Future Stars Theatre Arts, The Academy Performing Arts School, Matt Harrison, Harper James, Elliot Rodriguez, Rob Tofield, Leejay Townsend, Haydn Whiteside, Luke Barnes, Asha Reid, Pooja Ghai, Kerry Michael, Theatre Royal Stratford East, Claire Saddleton, The Arts Council, Galop, Theatre Delicatessen, Simon and How, Holly Easton, Paul Branghan, Debra Baker, Danny Kirrane, David Mumeni, Jacob Beswick, Sam Bradshaw, John Gordon, Sam Jackson, Emily Ross, Carlie Golding, Rosamund Hall, Dan Ainsworth, Eleanor Lawrence, Lisa Wagener, Hayley Crisp, Claire Archibald, Reece and Hazel Donn, Charlie Bland, Janice and Reg Bland, Antonia De Feo, Tracey Thompson, Maria Baker, Heather Leigh, Mark Williamson, Glenn Lee Stavers, Jennifer Armond, Jeylan Lyons, Olivia and Sonny Pearce, Nicola Ware, Lisa Woo, Scott Williams, Rosemarie Christian, Lucy Bull, Marie Manning, Louise Pope, Elise Cockley, Laura Morgan, Linda Jennings, Trev and Deb Manning, Steph Martin, Trevor Varian, Marcus Ellard, Charlotte Sterling, Angeline Bell, Tracey Tyer, Elliot at Playdead Press, Fabio Santos, Jonny Siddall, Sally Polden, Sam Goodey, Redbridge Drama Centre, James and Rosie at Pearson Casting, Tilly Wilson and all at Chloe Nelkin Consultancy, Nic Connaugton, Ellie Simpson and everybody at The Pleasance Theatre. And finally Vicky, for allowing us to tell her story.

For Janice and Vicky

A friendship that weathers all storms

CALL ME VICKY

by Nicola and Stacey Bland

Based on a true story, '*Call Me Vicky*' is set between the years of 1980 and 1985 in a council flat in Elephant and Castle and 'The Golden Girl' club in Soho, London at the height of the '80s drag scene.

Characters in order of appearance:

SYLVIE: Late 40s Martin's mum, typical South London working class woman. Spends all her time in the flat. Sylvie is always smoking

DEBBIE: 20, Martin's best friend from Essex. She loves the excitement and glamour of the world she is involved in

VICKY (MARTIN): 20, South London. At the beginning of the play Vicky (Martin) has been seeing a psychiatrist for 6 months to start the transition process.

GABBY: Mid 20s, Prostitute, recovering drug-addict. Has a young son Billy who lives with her at the club

FAT PEARL: 40s, Drag Queen who also runs the club, Butch gay man, more builder than beauty.

SID: 18, Punk Rocker from Dagenham, a loner who is easily influenced and really wants to be in their world

DAVE: (Played as cast)

Scene 1: Sylvie's House

A high-rise front room in Elephant & Castle. The fire alarm is going off, SYLVIE has been cooking

DOORBELL

SYLVIE: (*smoking*) Alright, alright, I'm coming

She stops the alarm by waving a tea towel

Don't worry Martin, I'll get it

VICKY: (*o/stage*) Mum you've gotta stop-

SYLVIE: -Alright

She opens the door. DEBBIE is standing there

Debbie!! (*Hugs her*)

DEBBIE: Hi Sylv, you alright?

SYLVIE: Come in, sit yourself down

DEBBIE: Is he not ready yet? We're meant to be at The Golden Girl for 8

SYLVIE: Well you know that ain't gonna happen. If he's much longer you can go down Robin's and get me some smokes

DEBBIE: I thought you were trying to give up

SYLVIE: (*coughing*) I tried... Have a cider, he won't be too long

DEBBIE: Alright

SYLVIE: Don't know what you see in that club anyway. Bunch of misfits

Sylvie exits to the kitchen

DEBBIE: I like it, it's exciting. Beats a night out in Romford any day

SYLVIE: (*calling*) How you been then Deb? You look like you lost weight?

DEBBIE: Really? Don't know about that. I'm alright though thanks

SYLVIE: Everything ok with Gary?

DEBBIE: I'm meeting his mum on Saturday

SYLVIE: Ahh that's good

Sylvie enters with drinks, she hands Debbie a small cider

(*Calling*) Martin... Deb's here

VICKY: (*o/stage*) Alright Deb?

DEBBIE: Yeah, you alright?

VICKY: (*o/stage*) Come up if you want

SYLVIE: No, she's down here with me having a cider and a catch up

VICKY: (*o/stage*) How's Gal, Deb?

DEBBIE: I was just saying, I'm meeting his mum on Saturday

VICKY: Bloody hell! They're gonna love you

DEBBIE: Hope so

SYLVIE: Hair's looking nice Deb, you just had it done?

DEBBIE: Yeah, last week actually

SYLVIE: (*shouting*) Deb's has had her hair done Martin, looks really nice

VICKY: Well I'll see it in a minute won't I mum

SYLVIE: Very short though...kind of boyish

DEBBIE: Bloody hell thanks Sylv!

SYLVIE: It does really suit you though Deb. Saw Poofy John the other day

DEBBIE: Oh yeah, what did he have to say for himself?

SYLVIE: Not much, I walked straight past him

VICKY appears at top of the stairs. She is dressed in a white crop top, high-waisted blue Levi jeans and platforms. She has sewn feathers, sequins and beads into the shoulders of her top. She wears her long curly hair down, and for the first time has channeled the New Romantics make-up.

VICKY: So... how do I look?

DEBBIE: Wow, that's quite dramatic

SYLVIE: Dramatic, that's not a word I'd use

DEBBIE: No I love it, just wait till we get up Soho, everyone will be staring

SYLVIE: That's if you make it there, you'll get beaten up if you go out like that

VICKY: (*off-hand*) Lucky I don't give a shit what you think then mum. Hair's nice Deb.

SYLVIE: That kind of outfit may be fine with all the other freaks you hang about with in that place, down on that estate they're not so

	forgiving, and I don't want people knocking on my door
VICKY:	Oh give up I'll be fine, let them stare. Right lets get out of here

She hurries down the stairs while she still has the nerve, catches Debbie's hand and hurries her out. As they go:

SYLVIE: What time shall I expect you?

Vicky looks at Debbie and rolls her eyes

VICKY: Bye mum.

DEBBIE: Bye Sylvie.

Scene 2: The Golden Girl Club

The Golden Girl Club. It is set like a typical cabaret venue with a small stage surrounded by tables and chairs. It is packed. GABBY is on the phone. FAT PEARL is doing her opening number*.

*This is the Drag Artists own comedy act.

FAT PEARL: Welcome to The Golden Girl and everyone's favorite night 'VIVA LA DRAG'. The only place to be on a Thursday, with me your fabulous, feisty, feline host (*meow*) Fat Pearl. They say diamonds are a girl's best friend… but in here

ALL: We prefer a Pearl Necklace

Laughter

FAT PEARL: Now let me hear a scream from my gays

PUNTERS: *scream*

FAT PEARL: A scream from my guys

PUNTERS: *scream*

FAT PEARL: And a growl from my lesbians

PUNTERS: Oh give over, shut it, very funny etc.

Vicky and Debbie sneak in late

FAT PEARL: Right, I'm exhausted after that so I'll leave you with our resident band and I'll see you lovely lot in a bit.

*Fat Pearl leaves the stage. The band play **DIAMONDS ARE A GIRLS BEST FRIEND** over the following*

VICKY / DEBBIE: Alright Gabby

GABBY: Finally! What time do you call this? You know what Pearl's like

VICKY: I'm not working till tomorrow

DEBBIE: She's 24 hours early

GABBY: Funny, let's see if you're that brave when she comes over

VICKY: Yeah, Lets

DEBBIE: Anyway. How's you? How's Billy?

GABBY: Yeah he's really well, did I tell you I got him a little bike? We went round the park last week, he's nearly ready to have his stabilisers off

DEBBIE: No, that's brilliant, God he's growing up so fast. How old's he now?

GABBY: He's gonna be 5 soon

Beat

So what's this about you working reception?

VICKY: What about it?

GABBY: Pearl's tight as arseholes, you ain't gonna get much extra

VICKY: Beggars can't be choosers. I'm saving for me op

GABBY: You're really going ahead with it?

VICKY: Yeah course I am

GABBY: Good for you... just don't go getting them bigger than mine or I'll be pissed

VICKY:	Don't I know it
FAT PEARL:	So, what did you think? Shirley Bassey eat your heart out (*See's Vicky*) Who invited Boy George?
VICKY:	I was gonna say the same about you, thought it was Maisie Trollette when I walked in
FAT PEARL:	I can understand that, the crowd were screaming for more
VICKY:	I meant your face
FAT PEARL:	They love me in here
DEBBIE:	Who wouldn't, they've got nothing to compare you with
FAT PEARL:	Oh, Fuck off!
VICKY:	You're right Gab, she's on one tonight
GABBY:	I never said that!
FAT PEARL:	What time do you call this anyway? Don't forget who pays your wages
VICKY:	Like I said to Gab, I'm not working till tomorrow
FAT PEARL:	If you're here you're working, go and get me a drink
VICKY:	You better be paying me for this

Fat Pearl gives Vicky a fiver

FAT PEARL:	Without me you lot wouldn't know your arse from your elbow. I'm doing my new set tonight?

VICKY: About time you learnt a new song or two… now all you need is a new wig and you'll be 'Divine'

FAT PEARL: Fuck off, there's nothing wrong with my wig

VICKY: Turn around, look at the back Deb, it's all matted ain't it?

DEBBIE: (*laughs*) Bloody hell Pearl, when was the last time you brushed it

FAT PEARL: That's enough you lot, you're doing my head in.

VICKY: Deb get a seat, I'll go and get these drinks.

Vicky goes to the bar

GABBY: Fat Pearl can I have a quick word

FAT PEARL: You've got 5 minutes

Gabby and Fat Pearl sit. Debbie goes to find a seat

GABBY: I just wanted to talk to you about my money

Fat Pearl takes out a bag of Marijuana and starts to roll. Gabby watches

FAT PEARL: Gabby, Fat Pearl can only save what Fat Pearl gets given

GABBY: I know, and I'm grateful – all the girls are - but I'm trying to save everything I earn for Billy, I know it's not right bringing a kid up in this place. It's just temporary

FAT PEARL: Oh yeah, 'coz of course, Rob's leaving his wife.

Gabby looks hurt

FAT PEARL: Look (*picks up a scrap of paper*) this is what you've given me since the beginning of the year. £500.

GABBY: I could have sworn I earnt £500 last month

FAT PEARL: I'm not running a doss house Gabby

GABBY: I'm not saying that

FAT PEARL: You've got your rent for upstairs, and then I pay for all your food and drink in this place

GABBY: I am trying

FAT PEARL: You're constantly dipping into it for smack or some other rubbish…

GABBY: …That's not fair

FAT PEARL: I'm just saying it as it is

GABBY: But I've been clean for 3 months, you know how hard I'm trying

Vicky takes Debbie her drink.

FAT PEARL: And *you* know my feelings on having Billy here.

GABBY: I said it's just until Rob…

FAT PEARL: …Gabby if he really cared about you or Billy he'd have paid for somewhere else by now.

GABBY: Yeah, I know

FAT PEARL: We're only looking out for you doll

GABBY: It don't feel that way, I just wish…

FAT PEARL: …well wish in one hand and shit in the other and see what you get most of.

GABBY: It's just frustrating you know

FAT PEARL: I know darling (*smiles*) you'll get there

GABBY: Look maybe I could have a couple extra nights, singing you know

FAT PEARL: Yeah, maybe

GABBY: The punters seemed to like me

FAT PEARL: You certainly had their attention. Thing is Gab, the songs were a bit slow, a bit morbid

Vicky gives Fat Pearl her drink. She listens

GABBY: I can sing some upbeat ones. I bet we'd pack this place out if you did some advertising

FAT PEARL: Listen, I'll have a think I might be able to sort something out

GABBY: Thanks, I really appreciate it

FAT PEARL: (*writing something down*) Right, get going, you're seeing Mick at 9.30 and he's asked for you especially. There you go darling and be safe

Gabby goes to exit. Vicky runs after her

VICKY: Gab… make sure he doesn't do what he did last time

GABBY: He won't

VICKY: Well this is just incase

Vicky gives Gabby a Spray. Gabby has gone. Vicky approaches Fat Pearl

	Is it still okay to move in upstairs next month?
FAT PEARL:	If you can watch your tongue
VICKY:	I was only messing
FAT PEARL:	Good, your mum still driving you mad then?
VICKY:	Not half, just so many questions ain't it Deb?
DEBBIE:	She's just being a mum
VICKY:	If you say so. As much as you lot drive me mad, I'll be happier when I'm living here
DEBBIE:	You'll miss her when you're gone
VICKY:	I know, but she's just so suffocating sometimes
FAT PEARL:	I know doll. Oh, Martin as you're here

Vicky goes to correct Fat Pearl then thinks better of it

	Will you do me a favour and pick one of the girls up for me?
VICKY:	If I have to
FAT PEARL:	You'd rather 'em safe. That's the address. I've got your money here for last week, do you need any or am I looking after it?
VICKY:	I'll take it, I need to start keeping track of what I'm saving

FAT PEARL: Whatever you want. Right I better get back to it

Fat Pearl walks back onto the stage. Vicky counts the cash, sits down and puts it in her bag.

> Welcome back saints and sinners now for my signature number ...hit it boys

I AM WHAT I AM

I am what I am
I don't want praise, I don't want pity
I bang my own drum
Some think it's noise, I think it's pretty
And so what if I love each sparkle and each bangle
Why not try to see things from a different angle
Your life is a sham
Till you can shout out
I am what I am

During the first verse of this number Vicky is quite still listening to the words Fat Pearl is singing. Vicky stands and grab's Deb's arm

VICKY: It's too loud in here, let's go outside

They hurry outside. The Club continues in the background

> *I am what I am*
> *And what I am needs no excuses*
> *I deal my own deck*
> *Sometimes the aces sometimes the deuces*
> *It's one life and there's no return and no deposit*
> *One life so it's time to open up your closet*
> *Life's not worth a damn till you can shout out*
> *I am what I am*

Vicky stands deep in thought as Deb rants

DEBBIE: I've gotta bring my own beans round to his mum's next week. I mean who goes round someone's for dinner and brings their own beans. I've never known anything-

VICKY: Will you start calling me Vicky?

DEBBIE: What?

VICKY: If you're not comfortable then…

DEBBIE: …No, it's not that… I'm just… you're actually doing this aren't ya?

VICKY: Yeah

They stand. Eventually

DEBBIE: It's exciting

VICKY: I was thinking more terrifying

DEBBIE: God you're brave, What's your Mum said?

The tempo changes and the song builds.

> *I am what I am*
> *And what I am needs no excuses*
> *I deal my own deck sometimes the aces sometimes the deuces*
> *It's one life and there's no return and no deposit*
> *One life so it's time to open up your closet*
> *Life's not worth a damn till you can shout out*
> *I am what I am*

SID runs down the alley and nearly bumps into Vicky and Debbie

VICKY: Whoa, watch where you're going

SID: Alright girls, don't suppose I could interest you in this state of the art, 8 track tape player...

VICKY: ...That you nicked

They laugh

DEBBIE: Well how much do you want for it?

SID: For you I can do a very good price

VICKY: No we're alright thanks

SID: You haven't even looked at it, come on, this is a one time opportunity

DEBBIE: Alright lets have a look

Sid puts the tape player in front of her, he watches her inspect it

VICKY: I like your top

SID: Oh, thanks, it's my favorite band

DEBBIE: I think you look cute (*referring to the tape player*) no thanks, not for me

SID: Well what about you? You got any tapes at home I could show you how it works

VICKY: You're forward

They laugh

SID: I didn't mean it like that

VICKY: I'm joking

SID: Right... I'll leave you to it then

DEBBIE: We're having a lock-in if you fancy a drink?

SID: (*To Vicky*) Only if you don't mind?

VICKY: Course not

*They re-enter The Golden Girl the after party is in full swing, **AINT NO MOUNTAIN HIGH ENOUGH** is playing they are drinking, dancing and doing lines of cocaine. Sid stands awkwardly on the periphery.*

FAT PEARL: Where have you two been? Come on you lot... shots

GABBY: I fucking hate shots

VICKY: Oh shut up and don't be a *wimp* (*To Sid*) and you, get over here

ALL: 1, 2, 3

They down the shots

GABBY: Who's your mate?

VICKY: Don't ask

SID: I'm Sid

GABBY: (*Looking at Vicky laughing*) God I love you

VICKY: I know

The Chorus Kicks in

GABBY: I love this song

VICKY: Turn it up

Gabby takes centre stage performing for her friends

GABBY: Look at me, I'm Fat pearl. They say diamonds are a girl's best friend

ALL: But in here we prefer a pearl necklace (*laugh*)

VICKY: Here, let me 'ave a go. What's the difference between a hooker and a drug dealer?

PUNTERS: I dunno, tell us etc

VICKY: A hooker can wash her crack and resell it!

They all laugh. Sid catches Vicky's eye and gives her an uncomfortable smile. She breaks the gaze. He drinks his beer

***DON'T GO BREAKING MY HEART** starts to play*

GABBY: What do the mafia and pussies have in common? One slip of the tongue and you're in deep shit.

VICKY: Gab, it's our song, come on

Don't go breaking my heart

She holds the mic to Gabby's mouth

GABBY: *I couldn't if I tried*

VICKY: *Honey if I get restless*

GABBY: *Baby you're not that kind*

VICKY: *Don't go breaking my heart*

GABBY: *You take the weight off me*

VICKY: *Honey when you knock on my door*

GABBY: *I gave you my key*

TOGETHER: *Nobody knows it*

The phone rings

FAT PEARL: Oi Gabby, it's for you

Gabby walks to the phone on the wall. The music continues in the background. Vicky is in her element now, singing along to the track, she has a good singing voice.

> *When I was down*
> *I was your clown*
> *Nobody knows it*
> *Right from the start*
> *I gave you my heart*
>
> *I gave you my heart*
> *So don't go breaking my heart*
> *I won't go breaking your heart*
> *Don't go breaking my heart*
> *And nobody told us*
> *'cause nobody showed us*
> *And now it's up to us babe*
> *I think we can make it*
> *So don't misunderstand me*
> *You put the light in my life*
> *You put the sparks to the flame*
> *I've got your heart in my sights*

GABBY: Hello, kingdom of the golden cunt, head pussy speaking? Rob, sorry, I thought you were one of the girls (*mouths and gestures be quiet to the club but Vicky takes that as excuse to go bigger*) don't talk to me like that...he is. Asleep upstairs. I don't have to explain myself to you. No, you listen to me. You can talk you barely see him. If you really cared you'd have left her by now

Vicky is now singing in front of Gabby, being silly trying to get her to loosen up and join in, Vicky is in her element. Vicky tries to take the phone to hang up but Gabby pushes her out of her face

GABBY:	We're just your dirty little secret, bet all of your mates fucking love that don't they. I don't want your money. You promised you'd look after us. I'm not on anything. I'll do anything for that boy. No. Fuck you Rob, Fuck you
FAT PEARL:	I hate to say it, looks like we've found our newest headliner
VICKY:	Oh I couldn't
DEBBIE:	Course you could
VICKY:	You're right I could
FAT PEARL:	Let's get you up here one night and see how you get on, and I'm not paying you for it

They laugh, 'tight bastard' 'course you won't' etc

VICKY:	Aright I will. Now turn that music up!

*Montage of music, strobing, drinking as the party grows and then dies again **IT'S TOO LATE** by Carole King plays*

SID:	I didn't catch your name earlier?
DEBBIE:	It's Debbie
SID:	And your mate?
DEBBIE:	…Vicky
SID:	Is she seeing anyone?
DEBBIE:	Not at the minute, why?
SID:	I was thinking of maybe asking her out for a drink?
DEBBIE:	Really? You fancy her?

SID:	Yeah, she seems nice
DEBBIE:	Oh. (*backtracks*) 'Coz if you don't I don't want you fucking her around
SID:	It's only a drink, but yea she seems like a laugh
DEBBIE:	Go for it… good luck

He walks away

Vicky sits at a table and unwraps heroin. She starts to put a small amount onto a square of tin foil. Sid approaches

VICKY:	What you doing lingering like a bad smell?
SID:	What?
VICKY:	Nothing, want some?

Sid shakes his head and looks away, he is clearly uncomfortable. Vicky puts it down on the table

VICKY:	(*Embarrassed*) It's only a bit of fun

Sid continues to stand there

VICKY:	Cat got your tongue?
SID:	Uh… no… I… er, wondered if you wanted to go for a drink
VICKY:	Well it's a bit late now ain't it?
SID:	No, I meant sometime, like another time, when you're free?
VICKY:	I'll have to check me diary

Gabby returns from the call, walks over to Vicky and grabs the foil and lighter from the table

GABBY: Let me have some

She lights underneath it

VICKY: Gab

GABBY: Don't

VICKY: I'm just looking out for you

GABBY: I know

She walks off to sit with Debbie. She inhales the fumes, Debbie sits awkwardly, unsure what to say. Eventually

DEBBIE: *You alright Gab?*

GABBY: I just want to bring Billy up like a normal kid

Debbie nods. A little confused by the outburst.

Be there for him after school, cook him dinners, you know, normal things

The heroin takes hold of Gabby

Coz that's all he needs Deb, and I'm trying, fuck, I'm trying. I'll get there, I have to

Gabby goes into a heroin coma. Debbie takes her coat off and puts it over Gabby. She sips her drink.

Scene 3: Sylvie's House / The Club Dressing Room

Vicky is at home getting ready for her first night of drag. We see her change from her previous outfit and replace that with a dress, stockings, suspenders and heels. She is removing the white face makeup and replacing it with bronzer, blush and red lipstick. Gabby and Fat Pearl are doing their make up at the club.

Sylvie enters with her pie 'n' mash on a tray. She is smoking

SYLVIE:	That boy called again, just as I was popping out to Robin's to get some smokes.
VICKY:	Mum leave it out, I'm not interested
SYLVIE:	Might be nice for you to have someone to go out with, to look after you
VICKY:	I don't need looking after (*she faces her mum*) and anyway you haven't met him, he's a wimp
SYLVIE:	Bloody hell what have you come as?
VICKY:	It's my first drag tonight ain't it?
SYLVIE:	What?
VICKY:	I thought I told you
SYLVIE:	I'm your bloody mother, I don't get told anything
VICKY:	Oh well, you know now

She finishes her make up

SYLVIE:	That club. I'm disgusted if I'm honest, I never thought you'd go down this road. Poofy John said…

VICKY: …Well Poofy John says a lot of things Mum. I love it, and everyone's really excited

SYLVIE: But you're saving for your op, don't you want to be taken seriously. I thought you was gonna wait and do it proper, not be like all them other gays playing dress up

VICKY: I'm not gay

SYLVIE: A man who fancies another man is gay and that's that

VICKY: Calm down. It's only a bit of fun

SYLVIE: There's a protocol you have to go through with these things Martin, you'd do well to remember that. They don't just let anyone do it

VICKY: Don't you think I know that, it's just some extra cash

SYLVIE: All you've been doing for the last 6 months could go to shit if your psychiatrist thinks it's a joke

Beat

VICKY: You know it's not a joke Mum. I could die from this op

SYLVIE: Don't say that

VICKY: Don't you think I'm scared

SYLVIE: You and me both

Sylvie continues to eat

You've always been special

VICKY: You mean feminine

Beat

I am serious about this mum

SYLVIE: I know you are. I'm alright with it love, but not everyone else is

VICKY: You do believe I was born in the wrong body, right?

SYLVIE: I'm your mother, of course I do

VICKY: Really?

SYLVIE: I mean you're one of five how could I not notice anything?

VICKY: You've got a point

SYLVIE: There was this one time, you must have been about 4, and your dad was adamant there was something wrong with you. Kept going on about taking you to the psychiatrists and making sure we did something. 'He's not like a proper boy' he'd say, 'let's get it sorted before he gets older and we can't do anything about it'

VICKY: That doesn't surprise me

SYLVIE: So I went along with it. We took you to the doctors. The lady was really nice, took you over to the kids play area and told you to play with whatever you wanted, and that we'd be over here talking to her. Well you weren't stupid, you got stuck in playing with the army figures, the trucks and the cars

VICKY: (*Laughs*) Course I did

SYLVIE: Well I had to laugh, I knew what you was up to, but sure as anything the doctor told us you was fine and a 'normal boy' and that was that. Your dad was not happy

Sylvie continues eating her pie 'n' mash. Vicky enters the club

VICKY: It's only me (*she grabs her fur scarf from the chair*)

FAT PEARL: Mart have you seen my wig, I'm sure I left it here last night

VICKY: 1. It's Vicky and 2. No

FAT PEARL: Oh sorry, I've gotta get used to that

VICKY: It's alright, so has everyone

GABBY: It will be easier once you start dressing more like "Vicky"

VICKY: (*laughs*) What's this "Vicky" gonna dress like then?

GABBY: Oh you know a bit more glamorous. I could always give you some help

VICKY: Let's get this right, on stage I'm gonna be 'Stiletto Express', then off stage I am Vicky, the only thing that's gonna change is I'm gonna have a pair of tits and no cock

FAT PEARL: Or you could be like me and have me both

VICKY: The difference between you and me is I was born in the wrong body and you're just fat

FAT PEARL: Alright keep your hair on Queen Victoria

VICKY: Oh shut up, and thanks for the extra shifts you promised, working that one shift on reception has made a huge difference to my savings

FAT PEARL: Don't start that, there's loads of ways of making money, you've just got to look further than your nose. God you lot would let me wipe your arse if you could get away with it

VICKY: If we weren't here to do your dirty work…

FAT PEARL: …If it weren't for me you'd see no way out of living with mummy and daddy in that council flat down the Elephant, you'd do well to remember that

GABBY: Oh shit, is this it Pearl?

She pulls the wig out from under her chair. Fat Pearl grabs the wig and puts it on.

FAT PEARL: Let's go.

Fat Pearl & Vicky go into the club. Gabby racks up a line of cocaine.

And now for 1 night and 1 night only I give you Stiletto Express 'A star is born'

AINT NO MOUNTAIN HIGH ENOUGH

VICKY:
> Listen baby, ain't no mountain high
> Ain't no valley low, ain't no river wide enough baby
> If you need me call me no matter where you are
> No matter how far don't worry baby
> Just call my name I'll be there in a hurry
> You don't have to worry

*'Cause baby there ain't no mountain high enough
Ain't no valley low enough
Ain't no river wide enough
To keep me from getting to you babe*

*Remember the day I set you free
I told you you could always count on me darling
From that day on, I made a vow
I'll be there when you want me
Some way, some how*

*'Cause baby there ain't no mountain high enough
Ain't no valley low enough
Ain't no river wide enough
To keep me from getting to you babe*

*Oh no darling
No wind, no rain
Or winters cold can stop me baby, na na baby
'Cause you are my goal
If you're ever in trouble
I'll be there on the double
Just send for me, oh baby, ha*

*My love is alive
Way down in my heart
Although we are miles apart
If you ever need a helping hand
I'll be there on the double
Just as fast as I can*

*Don't you know that there
Ain't no mountain high enough
Ain't no valley low enough
Ain't no river wide enough
To keep me from getting to you babe*

*Don't you know that there
Ain't no mountain high enough*

Ain't no valley low enough
Ain't no river wide enough
Ain't mountain high enough
Ain't no valley low enough

Fat Pearl walks over to Vicky and hands her a slip of paper

FAT PEARL: Here, details for tonight

VICKY: I thought I was done with that

FAT PEARL: One last time, then you'll get your money

*Vicky takes the paper and walks outside. Sid is waiting by the door. The club continues in the background as **YOUNG HEARTS RUN FREE** by Candi Staton plays*

SID: Alright Vick?

VICKY: Bloody hell Sid, scared me half to death. Sorry, you've caught me at a bit of a bad time I'm...

SID: ...busy, story of my life, I always seem to be doing that

VICKY: Don't be like that

SID: Are you ever gonna let me take you for a drink or am I just wasting my time?

VICKY: Look Sid, I'm not who you think I am

SID: Who is?

VICKY: I'm complicated

SID: One drink and then if you still aren't interested I promise, I'll leave you alone?

VICKY: Alright, we'll go for a drink, but not now, look I really am in a rush. Come to the club

	tomorrow and we'll go out after my shift, yeah?
SID:	Sounds good to me

Vicky has already started walking into the club

> (*shouting*) Have a good night

Vicky walks back into the club. Debbie and Gabby are sitting waiting for her

GABBY:	Was that that guy again?
VICKY:	Sid, yeah
DEBBIE:	He's not giving up is he?
VICKY:	(*Ignoring her*) Deb I'm working tonight now, I've gotta pick up one of the girls and then I'm off clipping
DEBBIE:	Clipping?

Gabby and Vicky share a knowing smile. Gabby grabs the scarf from Vicky's neck

GABBY:	So imagine I'm standing on a corner somewhere
VICKY:	Its gotta be out of the way from the busy streets
GABBY:	And then imagine Vicky, you're the bloke walking down the street

Vicky takes on the 'punter' persona and walks down the road grabbing 'himself'. Gabby responds in an overtly sexual manner

> Hello handsome

| **VICKY:** | Alright darling |

GABBY: Looking for a good time?

VICKY: What have you got in mind?

GABBY: Well... I was thinking... maybe...

VICKY: You've gotta make them think you're on the game

GABBY: Let's get a hotel and take it from there... what do you say?

VICKY: If they agree, once they've given you the money you arrange to meet later...

GABBY: ...But you don't turn up

DEBBIE: And they actually fall for it?

GABBY: They're too embarrassed to go to the police

VICKY: So voila you've got yourself 35 quid

Gabby looks at her watch

GABBY: Shit. I've gotta go... see you girls later

VICKY: Er... Gab, aren't you forgetting something

Vicky holds out her hand. Gabby takes off the scarf and exits

She'd have had that if I wouldn't have noticed. Look what I made last night

She empties her bag onto the table

DEBBIE: Wow. From clipping?

VICKY: Gotta be careful though, change areas every day just to make sure you don't get caught out. I got you a little something too, you're gonna love it

She goes to search in her bag

DEBBIE: Why don't Gabby do this?

VICKY: Debbie, it takes a certain sort of person to do this kind of work. You've either got it or you ain't

DEBBIE: She could use the extra cash

VICKY: She would have said if she was interested

DEBBIE: I'm not sure, she thinks that Fat Pearl's keeping more of a cut than she should be

VICKY: I thought the same the other month, so I've been holding onto all of mine ever since

DEBBIE: She wants to jack it all in and give Billy a normal family life. Well you know what I mean

VICKY: It must be hard for her

DEBBIE: Well the drugs don't help, I hope you're not encouraging her, she was doing so well before

VICKY: Course I'm not

Beat

Well, Do you wanna see what I got ya then or what?

Vicky reveals a vintage sequined dress she has bought Debbie

DEBBIE: Oh my god Vic you shouldn't have

VICKY: Well I know it's your and Gal's anniversary this weekend, and I wanted you to have something fabulous to wear

DEBBIE: What, down the legion

VICKY: He's not gonna take you there?

DEBBIE: Right, I'm off I'll see you tomorrow

VICKY: Shit I can't now, I said I'd meet Sid after work

DEBBIE: You've actually committed to a date?

VICKY: It's not a date, it's a drink

DEBBIE: Whatever you say

Scene 4: The Pub

Sid waits with flowers

VICKY: Sorry I'm late. You ain't been here long have you?

SID: I thought you'd stood me up... these are for you

VICKY: You shouldn't have... thanks

SID: Got you a drink. Weren't sure what you wanted

VICKY: This is fine

SID: It's a Campari and lemonade

They drink their drinks

So...

VICKY: So...

SID: What's new?

VICKY: Too much for a first date. You?

SID: I've got a trial on a building site next week

VICKY: Exciting, I thought stolen tape players were more your thing

SID: No. I was just earning a bit of extra cash. I don't normally do that kind of thing

VICKY: Alright, I believe you

They smile, both visibly nervous

Not nervous are you Sid?

SID:	No, no

Beat

VICKY:	I know nothing about you
SID:	What do you want to know?
VICKY:	Well I don't know, tell me something
SID:	I love Punk Rock
VICKY:	Never!

Beat

SID:	I've always liked photography
VICKY:	You got a camera?
SID:	Yea, but it's a crappy one. I'm thinking if I work on the site for a bit then I can save up and get a better one. I know, it's not as glamorous as your life, but I'm happy with a simple one
VICKY:	Me too

Beat

	What?
SID:	Nothing... you just look beautiful tonight

Vicky blushes

	Sorry, I didn't mean to embarrass you
VICKY:	It's fine, I'm just…
SID:	You're different
VICKY:	(*Dismissively*) I know I'm different

SID: I've never met anyone like you

VICKY: That's because you've never met-

SID: -It's not that. I can't put my finger on it. But I think it's great what you doing Vic

Beat

I know I probably shouldn't ask this, but how did you know?

Beat

Shit… too much for a first date?

VICKY: I think you're the first person to actually ask me that. I don't know, I've just always known

SID: But how did you know it was more than just doing drag?

VICKY: I've always known I was a woman, drag came after

SID: You're so pretty

VICKY: Right on that note shall we get some shots?

SID: I'll go

Sid goes to the bar Vicky unscrews her necklace containing cocaine and after making sure she's out of view taps some onto her hand does it. She checks herself in the mirror and reapplies her lipstick

Here we go, get it down ya

VICKY: What is it?

SID: Whiskey. Cheers

They do the shot

VICKY: Do you want some?

She passes her necklace across the table. Her hand brushes his, their eyes meet, they hold the stare.

SID: Shall we get out of here, I've got drink at mine?

VICKY: Yeah, alright then

They stand to go. Vicky staggers

SID: You alright?

VICKY: I don't know, I've got pins and needles in my legs, I think I might need to sit down

She falls to the floor and starts to have a severe epileptic fit

SID: Shit. Vic. Are you alright. Someone help. Vic can you hear me. Can someone call 999, I think she's having a fit

Scene 5: Sylvie's House

Sylvie is on the phone to the doctor from the hospital. She is smoking

SYLVIE: Is he alright? He wasn't alone was he? Well what's happened? Isn't he too old to get that now? Triggered by what? Lifestyle choices? What kind of substance abuse? He's not gay. Do you know how ridiculous that sounds? Let me stop you right there, believe me this is not a phase and it's certainly not a "popular" option. He's not confused, surely you can see on his file that's he's taking them hormone tablets? Don't you think we know the complications, he hasn't just…

So you're saying because he's gay he got epilepsy? Fine, ok. Shouldn't you be keeping him in over night? Whatever you thinks best. Right, thanks Doctor…

Vicky appears at the doorway. Sylvie hasn't noticed

Oh and by the way… it's not Martin, it's Vicky

Scene 6: The Street

Vicky enters carrying lots of shopping bags Gabby follows behind with two coffees. She puts the change from the coffees into Vicky's hand. Vicky fumbles her purse open

GABBY: What's that picture?

VICKY: Nancy

GABBY: Who?

VICKY: From Oliver, what's wrong with it?

GABBY: Vic you make me laugh! Only you would have a picture of that in your purse.

VICKY: She's my inspiration (*She holds it up*)

Can't you see the similarities?

GABBY: I'm so glad I got you out today, see it wasn't too bad was it

VICKY: It's been just what I needed, I've spent so much

GABBY: Yeah, but you needed to get some new outfits now Fat Pearls given you that slot back

VICKY: You're right. I'm not gonna get the big money if I look like shit

GABBY: I know, look at Pearl

They laugh

VICKY: Thanks Gab, I needed this

GABBY: Good to see you back on your feet

Beat

                I'm knackered, and I've gotta work tonight

VICKY: Call in sick, let's have a night out

GABBY: I'd love to but I've got a child to pay for remember

VICKY: How you ever gonna meet anyone if you're always working

GABBY: I probably won't

VICKY: Well, if the worse comes to worse Ill marry you but I ain't doing any of that other stuff

GABBY: (*Laughs*) You say that like it's a bad thing

VICKY: You're working too much lately

GABBY: I'm a grafter ain't I?

VICKY: Seriously though gab, if you're ever stuck you only need to ask right?

GABBY: Honestly, I'm fine. Don't worry about me, you've got enough to save for

VICKY: But I do worry about you, everyone needs someone to worry about

GABBY: I love you

VICKY: Good. And I know sometimes it's easier to get things off your chest with someone you don't know that well like Deb the other night, but...

GABBY: ...I ain't spoke to Deb

VICKY: Ok. Just saying you can always speak to me

GABBY:	To be honest I don't remember speaking to anyone that night
VICKY:	I thought you were doing alright
GABBY:	I was. I've gotta give up waiting for him ain't I?
VICKY:	I can't tell you what to do, but you've gotta start making Billy your main priority again
GABBY:	I know. I will. He's getting to an age where he's gonna remember me as a crack head, off her face you know
VICKY:	Don't say that. You do everything for that boy, you'll get back on track
GABBY:	I won't have him taken away from me. You know how much I love him Vic, I need to get clean for his sake. I just feel so trapped
VICKY:	Well, then, let me help you. I know you'll think I'm mad but take this

Vicky gets a wad of cash out of her bag

GABBY:	No, Vicky, I can't
VICKY:	A thank you, for always being there
GABBY:	I'm not a charity case
VICKY:	I know you're not
GABBY:	I can't take your money it's for your surgery
VICKY:	I've got enough
GABBY:	No you haven't

VICKY: But there's only one of me. There's a couple of months' worth of rent there plus some extra on top. Take it. Get yourself out of that bloody club it's no place for a child

GABBY: I can't

VICKY: Honestly, take it, for Billy's sake

Beat. She takes the money.

Scene 7: Sylvie's House

Vicky is at her mums. They are sat in front of the TV watching the Top of the Pops eating Pie 'n' Mash. Sylvie is smoking.

TV: *'Did you think I'd crumble, did you think I'd lay down and die'?*

BOTH:

> *Oh no not I, I will survive*
> *Oh as long as I know how to love*
> *I know I'll stay alive*
> *I've got all my life to live*
> *I've got all my love to give and I'll survive*
> *I will survive, Hey! Hey!*

Sylvie has a little coughing fit. Vicky rolls her eyes. The music continues in the background, as they watch

SYLVIE: So, tell me all about this new friend of yours

VICKY: There's nothing to tell, he's just a friend

SYLVIE: Alright, alright if you say so

She continues to eat

That's not what Deb said

VICKY: What did Deb say then?

SYLVIE: That you met him the other month at the club and I know he likes you coz he's rung here a few times

VICKY: Good old Deb

SYLVIE: Anyone's gotta be better than that bloody Millwall Kevin you went with, if I never see him again it'll be too soon

VICKY: You've got nothing to worry about there then, Sid's a wallflower in comparison

SYLVIE: Well, I look forward to meeting him then

DOORBELL

Ohhh

Sylvie puts her tray down on the table and goes to stand.

Vicky puts her tray down.

VICKY: No you're alright mum, save your legs, I'll go

SYLVIE: You're a good boy

Vicky rolls her eyes. She answers the door. Its Fat Pearl (dressed in jeans, wife-beater t-shirt, jacket & knackered reebok classics)

VICKY: Pearl. You alright? What's wrong? Come in, sit down

FAT PEARL: I'll stand thanks... bicycle accident

Vicky looks at Pearl in disbelief

VICKY: Um, ok. Well come on spill the beans, it must be big if you've come all the way down here to see me

Fat Pearl walks into the living room. This is the first time Sylvie has met anyone from the club, she is surprised at how "normal" he looks.

SYLVIE: Alright

FAT PEARL: Sorry to intrude... I didn't want to ring, it's Gabby

VICKY: Is she alright?

FAT PEARL:	She OD'd
VICKY:	No
FAT PEARL:	Vicky I'm so sorry
VICKY:	Don't tell me Billy was with her?
FAT PEARL:	Yeah, they were at home
VICKY:	Fuck
FAT PEARL:	I've been trying to get hold of his dad, he'll have to go there for the time being
VICKY:	I only saw her yesterday and she was fine, saying she wanted to start over
FAT PEARL:	Yeah, well, maybe she did
VICKY:	I gave her money
FAT PEARL:	You gave her money
SYLVIE:	You ain't got money to give
VICKY:	I don't understand
FAT PEARL:	She's not someone you can trust with money, you know that
VICKY:	She seemed fine
SYLVIE:	Of Course she did

Vicky darts Sylvie a look

	There's no point trying to understand it Mart
VICKY:	- For Fuck's sake mum, it's Vicky!

Scene 8: A Street

SID: We could go and see your sister in Devon for a few days, get out of London, we could both do with the break

Beat

You're mum even said she'd pay for the train tickets, thought that was –

VICKY: So you've been talking to my mum about me then

SID: No Vic, we're just worried about you

VICKY: Well don't be, I don't need -

SID: - Looking after, yeah I know that. But I just thought it would do us good to get away, see the kids

VICKY: You go then if you need the break so much

SID: Don't be like that, I thought you loved it down there

VICKY: No you love it down there, you get me all to yourself

SID: I can't say or do anything right when you're like this. I'm only trying to fucking help, I don't know why I bother

VICKY: Well don't I haven't asked you to

The Club

FAT PEARL: If she can't turn up for her shift then she'll lose it. I'm not running a doss house. She knows that

Sylvie's House

DEBBIE: I haven't spoken to her in days

SYLVIE: Neither have I Deb

DEBBIE: Will you call me when she turns up

The Street

SID: Is that what you want? You want me to walk away? Fine

Sid leaves Vicky sitting alone. She takes out a bottle of Vodka from her bag and drinks over the following.

Scene 9: The Golden Girl

DREAM A LITTLE DREAM OF ME by Doris Day plays faintly in the background. Debbie and Fat Pearl enter

DEBBIE: Nice of you to do the wake here. Pearl you spent the whole morning doing that makeup. And now it's halfway down your face. You've gotta stop crying you're meant to be hosting this

FAT PEARL: I can't help it, I'm just really emotional today

DEBBIE: You were so loud singing them hymns, everyone was looking

FAT PEARL: I was doing it for Gab, she always loved my voice

DEBBIE: Someone had to, and take that bloody veil off, you're not in the church now

Fat Pearl takes the veil off, still crying

FAT PEARL: Its times like this I feel a real connection with the Lord, I should get back into it

DEBBIE: Christ Pearl, going to the church doesn't make you a Christian anymore than standing in a garage makes you a car. Shall I get us a drink?

FAT PEARL: I'll have me usual. Billy seems to be doing alright with his Dad, didn't he do well doing that poem, it broke my heart

DEBBIE: Yeah. You'll have to get a copy, put it up in the club in memory of her

FAT PEARL: Don't be so insensitive Deb

DEBBIE: What?

FAT PEARL: You can't have something to do with the church in a place like this, it's disrespectful

DEBBIE: Oh I forgot you've come as a born again Christian today... we are not worthy

FAT PEARL: Oh piss off

They drink their drinks

FAT PEARL: I can't believe Vicky weren't there. I want her to be ok but this is taking the piss

DEBBIE: You don't need to go to church to pay your respects, you should know that

FAT PEARL: So you've heard from her then?

DEBBIE: No but-

FAT PEARL: Bet she feels terrible, it's no secret she gave Gabby all that money

DEBBIE: She weren't to know what she'd spend it on

FAT PEARL: Come on, don't play the fool

Silence. They drink their drinks

DEBBIE: It's not been the same without her around

FAT PEARL: Let's raise a glass to our Gabby, coz really it could have been any of us

They clink glasses

Scene 10: The Street

Vicky begins touting the passersby for business. A man walks past

VICKY: Alright gorgeous... want me to show you a good time?

He ignores her

Don't be shy... I'll do whatever you want

He walks off. Another man walks past

Alright darling, come on, spend your money on me

He ignores her and walks off. She gives up. Takes a swig from her bottle. She is physically exhausted and leans against the wall for support

She sees a man approaching and realises herself. She straightens up and sorts herself out

Alright gorgeous... you look like you could do with a girl like me

DAVE: Oh yeah?

VICKY: Let me show you a good time

DAVE: What did you have in mind?

VICKY: Well how about you tell me how much you've got and I'll tell you what you can afford...

DAVE: I'll have to stop you right there. I'm DC Cole and I'm arresting you on suspicion of importuning, you do not have to say anything unless you wish to do so but

>   anything you do say may be written down
>   and given as evidence. Do you understand?

VICKY: Fuck

DAVE: Now turn around

She turns

> Put your hands against the wall

She does, he slowly walks around her, trying to intimidate her. It works

> Now stand still

Vicky has instantly sobered up. Dave starts to frisk her, he feels her leg and as he travels up he works his way round to the front and grabs her crotch

> Well well well, what have we here?

VICKY: (*Winces*)

DAVE: You're a dirty...

VICKY: ...Please, don't hurt me

DAVE: You think that because you dress up like a girl I'll take it easy on you?

VICKY: No I was just...

DAVE: ...Don't you fucking dare talk back to me. You are a dirty piece of scum and someone needs to teach you a lesson

He pushes her onto the floor

> What's your name?

Silence

                        I said what's your name?

VICKY: Vicky

DAVE: What is it?

VICKY: Vicky

DAVE: Now, now, let's not play games *Vicky*, what's your fucking name

VICKY: Martin

DAVE: Martin what?

VICKY: (*hesitates*) Martin Wilson (*she cries*) Can't you just give me a caution... please

DAVE: A caution? Have a laugh. The chances are you've got previous and if I'm right, you're looking at doing some time. Some of the other coppers may be lenient with you lot but not me, and the men in those prisons won't be so kind to you neither. Now stand up

Vicky does not move

                        I said

He grabs her up

                        Stand up

He puts handcuffs on her

                        Stop crying you fucking nonce

He drags her off the stage.

Scene 11: Sylvie's House

Sylvie is on the sofa watching T.V. She is smoking. It's late. The Phone rings

SYLVIE: Hello?

VICKY: Mum, it's me

SYLVIE: Thank Christ for that...

VICKY: ...Look, I've gotta be quick I've only got a couple of minutes

SYLVIE: Where the hell are you? We've been...

VICKY: ...Worried sick, I know. Now Mum, I don't want you to panic but...

SYLVIE: ...Panic, how I can I not panic, I haven't been able to sleep for the last couple of nights. I've been sick to my stomach with worry

VICKY: Listen, I've been arrested. I got set up. An undercover cop jumped me whilst working

SYLVIE: Oh god

VICKY: I'll explain everything when I see you, now, I need you to do something for me, call Deb and get her to get me some stuff from the club

SYLVIE: What sort of stuff?

VICKY: Actually, I've probably got more... appropriate clothes at yours

SYLVIE: Like what?

VICKY: Clothes mum, I got arrested in my work clothes, and obviously I'm in a (*we hear the tremble/crack in her voice*) men's prison so I need men's clothes mum

Phone Beeps. Vicky's phone time is up

Fuck, my times up. Mum just call Deb and she will sort it all out with you. Try not to worry, Love you Mum

Phone beeps twice. The line goes dead. Sylvie stares blankly, trying to digest what's just happened.

SYLVIE: Love you Vic

Scene 12: The Prison

The visitor's room. Debbie enters with a tray of 2 teas and a bag of crisps. She sits at a table waiting for Vicky to arrive. She is nervous.

Vicky enters, apprehensive. She has been beaten up.

Debbie stands, they stand awkwardly for a second.

DEBBIE: I bought you a tea... I didn't know what you wanted

VICKY: Thanks for coming Deb

They hug

Don't cry

DEBBIE: What's happened to your face?

VICKY: It looks a lot worse than it is

DEBBIE: It's not drugs again is it?

VICKY: No

DEBBIE: I thought you were gonna keep your head down, stay out of trouble...

VICKY: It's not drugs

DEBBIE: It wouldn't be the first time though would it ...You're gonna send your mum to an early grave if you keep on like this

VICKY: Deb

DEBBIE: After all you've put her through

VICKY: You're not even listening

Beat

DEBBIE: I'm just worried about you that's all

VICKY: It isn't drugs

DEBBIE: Alright... If they're giving you a hard time Vic, tell someone

VICKY: There's no one to tell

DEBBIE: There must be someone

VICKY: Forget it

DEBBIE: No

VICKY: It's the screws; it was supposed to be for extra protection

DEBBIE: What was?

VICKY: They've been calling me out for Salvation Army visits

DEBBIE: I don't get it?

VICKY: Not the real Salvation Army... Deb just forget it

DEBBIE: No

VICKY: Fine... that's how they get you out of the cell, then the screws can do what they want to you

Beat

They raped me Deb. And I have to stand there while they decide who's turn it is. They don't get it, so this makes them feel better, like they know what I am, but they don't have a fucking clue. These happily married men with their perfect lives who really are so

	unhappy their only release is making my life a misery. They treat me like dirt Deb, and it's for my own good, apparently, to protect me.
DEBBIE:	It don't look much like protection, look at the state of you
VICKY:	But that's what they think of me, that's what everyone thinks of me, and they always will. I was stupid to think I could ever be seen as anything else.
DEBBIE:	I don't think that
VICKY:	Well you're one of the good ones Deb
DEBBIE:	How can they get away with it?
VICKY:	The screws don't care about me, they've never met people like me. I just can't wait to be out, if I make it out
DEBBIE:	Don't say that

Scene 13: The Golden Girl Club

Fat Pearl is onstage. Sid is now working at the Club, it is buzzing. Debbie enters the Club and finds Sid who is clearing a table.

I WILL SURVIVE

> *At first I was afraid, I was petrified*
> *Kept thinking I could never live without you by my side*
> *But then I spent so many nights thinking how you did me wrong*
> *And I grew strong*
> *And I learned how to get along*
>
> *And so you're back, From outer space*
> *I just walked in to find you here with that sad look upon your face*
> *I should have changed that stupid lock, I should have made you leave your key*
> *If I'd known for just one second you'd be back to bother me*
>
> *Go on now, go, walk out the door*
> *Just turn around now*
> *'Cause you're not welcome anymore*
> *Weren't you the one who tried to hurt me with goodbye*
> *Do you think I'd crumble*
> *Did you think I'd lay down and die?*
> *Oh no, not I, I will survive*
> *Oh, as long as I know how to love, I know I'll stay alive*
> *I've got all my life to live*
> *A*nd I've got all my love to give and I'll survive*
> *I will survive, hey, hey*

SID: How's she holding up?

DEBBIE: Looks like a bag of shit if I'm honest

SID: Any news on the release date?

DEBBIE: She's hoping to be out in the next few weeks, thank god

SID: I'd love to see her, did she say anything about me?

DEBBIE: Why else do you think I'm here?

SID: *Oh*
It took all the strength I had not to fall apart
Kept trying hard to mend the pieces of my broken heart
And I spent oh-so many nights just feeling sorry for myself, I used to cry
But now I hold my head up high
And you see me Somebody new
I'm not that chained-up little person and still in love with you
And so you felt like dropping in and just expect me to be free
Well, now I'm saving all my lovin' for someone who's loving me

The Club scene continues in the background

SYLVIE: Thanks for calling

VICKY: I just wanted to hear your voice

SYLVIE: I love you my darling girl

VICKY: Love you Mum

Go on now, go, walk out the door
Just turn around now
'Cause you're not welcome anymore
Weren't you the one who tried to break me with goodbye
Do you think I'd crumble
Did you think I'd lay down and die?

Oh no, not I, I will survive
Oh, as long as I know how to love, I know I'll stay alive
I've got all my life to live
And I've got all my love to give and I'll survive
I will survive, Oh

The Prison

VICKY: Is Fat Pearl coming?

DEBBIE: She's busy, she's got a club to run, you know what it's like. Anyway, you've only got two more weeks

VICKY: I know

DEBBIE: You've got this far, you'll be back home in no time

VICKY: Then that's it; I can't do it anymore. I've got to sort myself out, and if this place ain't a wake up call I don't know what is. I know what you're thinking Deb, but I'm serious

DEBBIE: I know you are

Go on now, go, walk out the door
Just turn around now
'Cause you're not welcome anymore
Weren't you the one who tried to break me with goodbye
Do you think I'd crumble
Did you think I'd lay down and die?
Oh no, not I, I will survive
Oh, as long as I know how to love, I know I'll stay alive

I've got all my life to live
And all my love to give and I'll survive
I will survive
Hey! Hey!

Scene 14: Outside the Prison

Debbie and Sid are waiting outside the prison.

It's Vicky's release day. Sylvie is running late.

SID: What's the time?

DEBBIE: 5 to

SID: God, I'm nervous

DEBBIE: Don't be silly, you'll be fine

SID: You sure this is the right place?

DEBBIE: Yes Sid

Beat

SID: What's the time?

DEBBIE: We've *still* got 5 minutes

SID: Ok

Beat. Debbie looks at Sid

DEBBIE: New top?

SID: What? Ah, no, I just thought…

DEBBIE: …No, I like it. Didn't think you had anything else, I've only ever seen you in that Sex Pistols t-shirt

SID: Vicky likes me in it… she said so

DEBBIE: What and so you've worn it ever since

Sylvie enters, she looks flustered, she is smoking

SYLVIE: Sorry I'm late, that bloody 133

DEBBIE: Don't worry Sylv

SYLVIE: Thank God I ain't missed it, you been here long?

DEBBIE: Not too long, about 10 minutes, got the tube

SYLVIE: Good. Glad to see you alive and kicking

DEBBIE: What?

SYLVIE: Poofy John only went and told me you were dead

DEBBIE: He really is a prize prick

SYLVIE: Course I didn't believe him

Beat

(*looking at her watch*) Should be out soon

Beat

DEBBIE: Oh, Sylvie, by the way, this is Sid

SYLVIE: Sid? Oh, about time

SID: Nice to meet you Mrs Wilson

SYLVIE: Call me Sylvie

SID: Nice to meet you Sylvie

Beat

SYLVIE: I thought about maybe Pie and mash on the way home? I bet she's dying for a decent meal. You like pie and mash Sid?

SID: Yeah, love it

SYLVIE: Well lets do that then, yeah Debbie? You ain't gotta rush back and do Gary's dinner have you?

DEBBIE: You sound like my bloody mother, poor old Gary! No, he can do it himself

Unnoticed Vicky enters and watches

SYLVIE: Well that's that then, anyone want a bonbon?

DEBBIE: Yea alright

SID: Err, yeah

Sid turns to get a sweet and notices Vicky. Vicky can't hide her delight that Sid is there waiting for her. A smile breaks across Sid's face. They share a moment

VICKY: I see you've met me mother?

Scene 15: The Golden Girl

Fat Pearl enters dressed as a Bride with a bouquet of flowers

LIKE A VIRGIN

>*I made it through the wilderness*
>*Somehow I made it through*
>*Didn't know how lost I was*
>*Until I found you*
>
>*I was beat, Incomplete*
>*I'd been had, I was sad and blue*
>*But you made me feel*
>*Yeah, you made me feel*
>*Shiny and new*
>
>*Hoo, Like a virgin*
>*Touched for the very first time*
>*Like a virgin*
>*When your heart beats*
>*Next to mine, like a virgin*
>
>*Gonna give you all my love, boy*
>*My fear is fading fast*
>*Been saving it all for you*
>*'Cause only love can last*
>
>*You're so fine, And you're mine*
>*Make me strong, yeah you make me bold*
>*Oh your love thawed out*
>*Yeah, your love thawed out*
>*What was scared and cold*
>
>*Like a virgin, hey*
>*Touched for the very first time*
>*Like a virgin*
>*With your heartbeat*
>*Next to mine*

Whoa
Whoa, ah
Whoa

You're so fine
And you're mine
I'll be yours
'Till the end of time
'Cause you made me feel
Yeah, you made me feel
I've nothing to hide

Like a virgin, hey
Touched for the very first time
Like a virgin
With your heartbeat
Next to mine
Like a virgin, ooh ooh
Like a virgin

Feels so good inside
When you hold me,
And your heart beats,
And you love me
Oh oh, ooh whoa
Oh oh oh whoa
Whoa oh ho, ho
Ooh baby
Yeah
Can't you hear my heart beat
For the very first time?

I AM WHAT I AM begins to play in the background over the following

FAT PEARL: Hello Ladies and Gents...and welcome to The Golden Girl and everyone's favorite night 'VIVA LA DRAG'. The only place to

	be on a Thursday, with me Pearl. They say diamonds are a girl's best friend... but in here.
ALL:	We prefer a Pearl Necklace

Laughter

FAT PEARL:	Now let me hear a scream from my gays
PUNTERS:	*scream*
FAT PEARL:	A scream from my guys
PUNTERS:	*scream*
FAT PEARL:	And a growl from my lesbians
PUNTERS:	Oh give over, shut it, very funny etc.
FAT PEARL:	I can see loads of friendly faces in the audience tonight... give us a wave Debbie?
DEBBIE:	Hello Pearl
FAT PEARL:	Sid, keep clearing them tables
VICKY:	Leave him alone
FAT PEARL:	Ah, not forgetting everyone's *second* favorite Queen... how's my gorgeous Vicky?
VICKY:	You feeling alright?
FAT PEARL:	Vic, on a serious note, it's really good to have you back with us, we've missed you. Now, enough of that don't want you thinking I'm soft. I've offered her slot back, but she's not interested, so for one last time I give you Stiletto Express. Vicky get up here

Fat Pearl and Vicky join in on the up tempo section of the song

I am what I am
And what I am needs no excuses
I deal my own deck
Sometimes the aces sometimes the deuces
It's one life and there's no return and no deposit
One life so it's time to open up your closet
Life's not worth a damn till you can shout out
I am what I am

Scene 16: Sylvie's house

Sylvie is sitting on the sofa with her oxygen mask on and tank next to her. Vicky is next to her. Her chest is bandaged up. They are watching the TV

SID: (*o/stage*) Only me

Sid walks in. Sylvie reaches to take her mask off

VICKY: No don't take it off mum

Sylvie takes it off. Gives out a small cough

SYLVIE: It's fine, I need a break. Doctor said I shouldn't rely on it too much or my lungs will get lazy

Sylvie lights up a cigarette

VICKY: Mum!

SYLVIE: I've been smoking since I was 13, if I stop now my lungs would go into shock

Vicky laughs

You laugh, I was watching TV-AM the other morning and some doctor was saying that giving up when you're older sometimes makes things worse. Releases negative emotions or something. You hear these stories all the time, she was 90 gave up smoking then pegged it. So what's the point, and I enjoy it!

Sid plonks "Woman's Weekly" magazine on Sylvie's lap

SID: I hope I got the right one

VICKY: Well your not 90 and anyway I'm not going there mum. You know my feelings on this and I'm not arguing with you today

SYLVIE: Makes a change

VICKY: Mum I don't always want to argue with you believe it or not. You just frustrate me sometimes

SYLVIE: Charming!

VICKY: The only reason you're on that (*pointing at the oxygen tank*) is because you're too busy running around for everyone else.

SYLVIE: No I'm not

VICKY: Maggie next door is younger than you but you're the one rushing here there and everywhere to get her shopping, prescription or her sons bloody birthday card! She's not ill mum she's FAT!!

SYLVIE: Sshh Vicky, she'll hear you!

VICKY: I don't care, I want you to be around for the next 50 years, see your grand kids grow up! The rate you're going you'll be in the grave in no time

SYLVIE: Thanks for that

VICKY: You know what I mean. When I got that phone call from the hospital it frightened the life out of me

SYLVIE: Well now you know how I felt when it used to be you

VICKY: Look after yourself mum, stop doing everything for everyone. You need to slow down a bit yeah? You're too precious to lose

Sylvie looks a little taken a back

SYLVIE: I'll slow down I promise

Beat

Sid, what's in that M&S bag, got us something nice for dinner?

VICKY: Sid, come and sit down

SID: I'm just making sure I got everything off the list

SYLVIE: (*Looking at the magazine*) That's the right one, thanks Sid, did Robin send his love?

SID: (*Laughs*) Have yous ever spoke to Robin

SYLVIE: Course, I've been buying me fags from him for the last 30 years

SID: So you know his name's not actually Robin?

SYLVIE: // Yeah

VICKY: // No

VICKY: What?

SYLVIE: Yeah. Course. We nicknamed him on the estate. 'Coz he's a robbing fucking bastard

VICKY: Mum!

They all laugh. Sid starts fussing around Vicky

SID: You comfortable?

VICKY: I'd be a hell of a lot more comfortable if you would stop trying to prop me up

SID: I'm sorry I was only trying to help

VICKY: I know but I'm not an invalid

SID: You've had a major operation

VICKY: How could I forget. Mum put that mask back on

He sits down beside her

SID: How are they looking?

VICKY: I don't know Sid, they're bandaged up aren't they. Your guess is as good as mine

SID: I just meant, I thought you were taking the bandage off today. How do they feel, any better?

VICKY: Fucking sore Sid, how do you think they feel?

SID: Alright

Beat

VICKY: Sorry

Beat

Pass the remote

SID: What do you want on?

VICKY: Not sure, I'll flick through and find something

SID: Alright (*he gives her the remote*)

Beat

     Shall I make you girls a cuppa?

VICKY: Oh yes please

Sid exits to the kitchen

SYLVIE: (*calling*) Maybe a couple of custard creams to go with it

Scene 17: The Park

Vicky & Debbie have met in the park. It's a bright day. They both have takeaway cups of tea from the Park tea hut.

VICKY:	You're pregnant?
DEBBIE:	Oh Vic, you've ruined it! Trust you to guess it!
VICKY:	Oh shit sorry! It just slipped out, I didn't think! Shit. Let's rewind, pretend I didn't say it!
DEBBIE:	Shut up, it's fine…
VICKY:	…Nope let's go again
DEBBIE:	Vicky!
VICKY:	Just say it again! Go on please… I've got something to tell you… go on
DEBBIE:	(*laughing, joining in with the silliness*) You're an idiot. Fine! I've got something to tell you…
VICKY:	…You're getting a divorce? You've won the pools?! Tell me tell me!
DEBBIE:	I'm pregnant!!

The girls laugh

VICKY:	Deb that is fantastic news! I'm so happy for you
DEBBIE:	It's early days but I just had to tell you. The scan's next week then we're gonna tell everyone. Just can't believe it, and we barely had to try!

The girls laugh

VICKY: Your mum must be so pleased

DEBBIE: Yeah she is. We only told her last night, wanted to be sure you know

There's a natural pause whilst they soak it all in. Drinking

VICKY: Well, whilst we are on good news

DEBBIE: What?

VICKY: I've been given the go ahead to finally transition

DEBBIE: Oh my god Vic

VICKY: I know! Psychiatrists are happy with my progress and where I'm at. I've been waiting for 2 years, and the NHS has finally given me a date

DEBBIE: That's such amazing news, I'm so happy for you

VICKY: I'm still trying to take it all in myself. That this is actually going to happen.

DEBBIE: You'll legally be Vicky Wilson

VICKY: Yeah I can get round to that. But I can start to live the life I'm meant to be living

Beat

Once this happens though Deb, I'm starting a fresh. I've seen too many people fuck it all up. I want a proper job, a shop job or something. Where no one knows about the past

DEBBIE: (*squeeze leg*) Good for you Vic

VICKY: I want for them to just know me as Vicky and for me and Sid to have a normal life just like everyone else

DEBBIE: It's not gonna be that easy you know

VICKY: I know, but it's a start. There's a new Safeway opening down the road from here. Might try there. It's all finally clicking into place Deb. I'll meet your gorgeous baby as Vicky and it won't know me as anything different.

Beat

This is it Deb. This is our year.

Vicky squeezes Debbie's hand. They look out over the park

Blackout

END